· WEIRD SCIENCE ·

FOOD

HOW THE HECK DOES THAT WORK?!

VIRGINIA LOH-HAGAN

45th Parallel Press

Published in the United States of America by Cherry Lake Publishing Group
Ann Arbor, Michigan
www.cherrylakepublishing.com

Reading Adviser: Beth Walker Gambro, MS, Ed., Reading Consultant, Yorkville, IL
Book Designer: Felicia Macheske

Photo Credits: © Yeti studio/Shutterstock, cover, 1; © Anastasiia Skorobogatova/Shutterstock, cover, 1;
© prapass/Shutterstock, cover, 1; © Valentina Razumova/Shutterstock, cover, 1; © Mark Herreid/Shutterstock,
cover, 1; © bestv/Shutterstock, cover, 1; © White ground/Shutterstock, cover, 1; © Shutter_M/Shutterstock,
cover, back cover, 1; © Epine/Shutterstock, cover, back cover, 19; © Andrei Kuzmik/Shutterstock, cover, back
cover, 1; © Lev Kropotov/Shutterstock, cover, back cover, 1; © akepong srichaichana/Shutterstock, cover, back
cover, 1; © NataLima/Shutterstock, cover, back cover, 1, 13, 19; © Markus Mainka/Shutterstock, back cover, 1;
© Tatjana Baibakova/Shutterstock, 4; © alex74/Shutterstock, 5; © RTimages/Shutterstock, 6; © ALPA PROD/
Shutterstock, 7; © gn fotografie/Shutterstock, 8; © SciePro/Shutterstock, 10; © Krakenimages.com/Shutterstock,
11; © Rob Marmion/Shutterstock, 12; © Yurii Andreichyn/Shutterstock, 14; © Eightshot Images/Shutterstock, 15;
© Andrey_Popov/Shutterstock, 16; © siamionau pavel/Shutterstock, 18; © Buntoon Rodseng/Shutterstock, 19;
© Iakov Filimonov/Shutterstock, 20; © Drawlab19/Shutterstock, 22; © SUPERMAO/Shutterstock, 23; © casanisa/
Shutterstock, 24; © Fine Art Studio/Shutterstock, 26; © CkyBe/Shutterstock, 26; © Yulia.Panova/Shutterstock, 27;
© Shine Nucha/Shutterstock, 28; © AYA images/Shutterstock, 30; © Milkovasa/Shutterstock, 31

45th Parallel Press is an imprint of Cherry Lake Publishing Group.

Library of Congress Cataloging-in-Publication Data

Names: Loh-Hagan, Virginia, author.
Title: Weird science : food / by Virginia Loh-Hagan.
Description: Ann Arbor, Michigan : Cherry Lake Publishing, 2021.
  | Series: How the heck does that work?! | Includes index.
Identifiers: LCCN 2021004939 (print) | LCCN 2021004940 (ebook)
  | ISBN 9781534187597 (hardcover) | ISBN 9781534188990 (paperback)
  | ISBN 9781534190399 (pdf) | ISBN 9781534191792 (ebook)
Subjects: LCSH: Food—Juvenile literature. | Food habits—Juvenile
  literature.
Classification: LCC TX355 .L67 2021 (print) | LCC TX355 (ebook) | DDC
  641.3—dc23
LC record available at https://lccn.loc.gov/2021004939
LC ebook record available at https://lccn.loc.gov/2021004940

Cherry Lake Publishing Group would like to acknowledge the work of the Partnership for 21st Century Learning,
a Network of Battelle for Kids. Please visit *http://www.battelleforkids.org/networks/p21* for more information.

Printed in the United States of America
Corporate Graphics

**Dr. Virginia Loh-Hagan is an author, university professor, and former classroom teacher.
She's currently the Director of the Asian Pacific Islander Desi American Resource Center
at San Diego State University. She loves eating food. She lives in San Diego with her very
tall husband and very naughty dogs.**

TABLE OF CONTENTS

Types of food include grains, fruits, vegetables, dairy, meats, nuts, and oils.

INTRODUCTION

All kinds of weird science can happen with food. Food scientists study food. They learn how food affects our bodies. They make food stay fresh for a long time. They make food taste good. They make food safe to eat. They improve food. They make new types of food.

Our bodies need food and water to live. Food gives us energy. We need energy to grow and work. Our mouths chew food. Food travels to the stomach. The stomach breaks down the food. It gets rid of human waste. It keeps what it needs for energy.

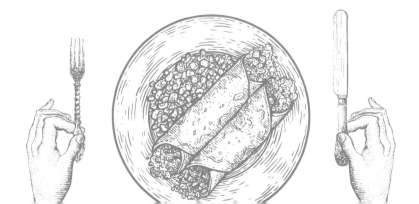

Food is everywhere. Early humans hunted for meat. They fished. They gathered plants. They ate what they found on the land. They learned how to cook over a fire. They learned to **preserve** food. Preserve means to save.

Today, we get most of our food from farms and stores. Food scientists and food companies provide food for us. Want to learn where your food comes from? Want to learn what food does to our bodies?

Dare to learn more about food science! So much is going on. How the heck does it all work?

Food science includes developing ways to preserve and store foods. This lets people save food to eat during the winter.

Sugar is sweet. Strawberry is a flavor.

CHAPTER 1

TASTING FLAVORS

How do you taste **flavors**? Flavor includes tastes, smells, temperature, and **texture**. Texture is how something feels. Tasting helps you survive. It helps you choose foods. It helps you avoid being poisoned.

There are 5 types of taste. They're sweet, sour, bitter, salty, and **umami**. Umami means savory or meaty. But there are a lot of smells. This means humans can taste about 100,000 different flavors.

Your teeth and jaw break down food when you eat. Food is broken into tiny bits. In the middle of your tongue, there's a dip. It fills with water. It detects food.

Some people are supertasters. They have extra papillae in their tongues.

Tongues have a lot of tiny bumps. These bumps are called **papillae**. Taste buds are inside the papillae. Adults have about 2,000 to 10,000 taste buds. The taste buds have many **sensory cells**. Sensory cells are renewed every 3 to 10 days. These cells have tiny tasting hairs. The hairs connect with nerve cells. These cells send messages to the brain. The brain identifies tastes.

The nose is also working when you eat. While you chew, food releases chemicals that travel up your nose. Sensory cells in noses and tongues work together. They send messages to the brain. The brain identifies flavors.

You might think you taste with your mouth. But you don't. You taste with your brain!

There are different types of artificial sweeteners. They're used for different purposes. For example, sucralose is used in baked goods. It can take heat.

CHAPTER 2

ARTIFICIAL SWEETENERS

Do you like to eat sweet things? Sweet things have sugar. Sugar has a lot of **calories**. Calories are units of energy. You need energy. But there needs to be balance. Eating too many calories in general can be bad. It can lead to health problems. Eating too much sugar also can be bad. It can make you sick. This is why people use **artificial sweeteners**. These are fake sugars. They add a sweet flavor. But they have fewer calories than real sugar.

Artificial sweeteners are used in many products. They're used in baked goods. They're used in sodas and candy. They're used in toothpaste. They're even used in medicine.

Even WEIRDER FOOD SCIENCE!

- Deep under Earth's surface is very hot. It has a lot of pressure. Diamonds are formed here. They're carbon atoms. They've been heated and squeezed. They're pushed to the Earth's surface, where they cool. Dan Frost is a German scientist. He's making fake diamonds. He tried to copy the extreme conditions. He used peanut butter in his tests. Peanut butter has a lot of carbon.

- The Boeing Company makes planes. Company workers were testing the planes' Wi-Fi. Instead of humans, they used potatoes. They put big sacks of potatoes on plane seats. Potatoes have a lot of water. They take in and reflect Wi-Fi signals just like humans.

- Most red food dye is made of carmine. Carmine is made from the cochineal bug. These bugs are dried and crushed. They're made into a powder. They're dunked into an acid solution. Solutions are liquid mixtures. About 70,000 bugs are needed to make 1 pound (0.5 kilogram) of dye.

Real sugar is taken in by the body. It's **digested** by the body. Digested means broken down. Then, sugars move into the bloodstream. The pancreas is a body organ that controls blood sugar levels. It releases special **hormones**. Hormones are made in the body and helps it grow and develop. These hormones absorb blood sugar or it releases stored sugar. This process helps keep a steady supply of blood sugar circulating throughout the body. This is what gives you energy!

Artificial sweeteners don't provide calories or **nutrients**. Nutrients include proteins and vitamins. They're like empty food. The pancreas can't do anything with artificial sweeteners.

Artificial sweeteners are sweeter than sugar. They can numb your taste buds. It can make you crave more sugar. It's better to eat more "real" calories than "fake" calories.

Real calories have nutrients. Fake calories don't.

Microwaves are like small ovens. They heat and cook food. Some food tastes better when heated.

CHAPTER 3

HEATING FOOD

Why do you need to heat food? Some food needs to be heated. Heat kills germs. It makes food safe to eat. Heating also makes food taste better. We heat foods over fires. We heat foods in ovens.

Heat is the **transfer** of energy from 1 thing to another. Transfer means to move. When 2 things touch, they transfer heat. Heat flows from hot things to colder things. In cooking, fire transfers its heat to food.

When sugar is heated, it melts. It turns into a liquid. The sugar browns. It **caramelizes**. This is the process of sugar breaking down into simpler sugars.

Plants and meats are made of proteins. These proteins are like coils. When they're heated, they unwind. They break up. Heat shrinks the muscle fibers. Water is squeezed out. Proteins **coagulate**. This means when liquids turn into solids.

Starches include pasta, rice, and potatoes. When heated, starches take in water. They swell. The glue that holds starches together breaks down. Starches get soft. They lose water. They turn into gel.

Water is made of **molecules**. Molecules are small units of a substance. When water is heated, molecules move faster. Then, they **evaporate**. Evaporate means to turn into a gas or steam. Fats don't evaporate like water. When heated, they melt.

Reheating food over and over makes it lose its flavor.

UNSOLVED MYSTERY

Anything that takes up space is matter. Dark matter is a type of matter. We can't see it. We don't know what it is. We just know it's there. Scientists say food has dark matter. No one knows exactly what our food is. All foods have compounds. We can identify many of the compounds. But there are many more compounds we don't know about. Food scientists are working to identify and record these compounds. They want to know which compounds make us sick. They want to know which compounds are good for us. For example, we know berries are good for us. But what exactly in berries makes them good? A scientist said, "Our understanding of how diet affects health is limited to 150 key nutritional components. But these represent only a small fraction of the biochemicals present in our food." Food scientists want to learn more.

Pickling can take hours, days, and sometimes months!
More soaking means more sourness.

CHAPTER 4

PICKLING FOOD

Have you ever eaten pickles? Pickles are **pickled** cucumbers. But you can pickle almost anything. Pickled foods are soaked in solutions. Pickling preserves foods. It keeps food from rotting. Pickling also changes the taste of foods.

Most pickled foods are preserved in water, salt, and **vinegar**. Vinegar is a strong acidic liquid. It causes the sour taste in pickles. It replaces the water in foods. Pickling increases the acidic levels of foods. This kills **bacteria**. Bacteria are tiny living things that exist all around us. They cause food to **decay**. Decay means to rot. Food begins to break down. Pickling with vinegar controls the decay. It slows down the decaying process.

TEST IT OUT!

Almost everybody loves ice cream. Ice cream is a mixture of milk, cream, and sugar. Learn about how ice cream works.

Materials

- Large container with lid
- Crushed ice
- Rock salt
- Gloves
- 2 large plastic zipper bags
- Cream
- Brown sugar
- Vanilla extract

1. Fill a large container half full of crushed ice. Add 6 tablespoons (89 milliliters) of rock salt. Seal tightly. Shake for 5 minutes. Wear gloves to keep your hands warm.

2. Fill a plastic bag with ½ cup (0.2 liter) of cream, ½ tablespoon (7.4 mL) of brown sugar, and 1 teaspoon (4.9 mL) of vanilla extract. Seal the bag tightly. Make sure there's no air. Put the bag into the other bag. Seal tightly so the salt won't get in.

3. Put the bag inside the salt container. Seal tightly. Salt lowers the melting point of ice. It draws heat out from the cream mixture faster. This makes the cream mixture freeze into ice cream.

4. Shake the container to mix the cream. Do this for 20 minutes. This churning makes sure hard ice doesn't form. It adds air. It makes the ice cream soft and creamy.

5. Take out the ice cream. Enjoy!

People follow a few steps to pickle food. First, the pickling solution is heated. The heat kills any bad bacteria. Then, the pickled food needs to be **canned**. To can foods means to seal tightly in jars or cans. This keeps out oxygen. Oxygen causes food to decay.

Pickled food can also be preserved in a **brine**. Brine means salt water. This type of pickling causes **fermentation**. The salt draws out water from the food. It keeps the food from decaying. It breaks down the food sugars. The sugars turn into lactic acid. This acid grows good bacteria. It pushes out bad bacteria.

Pickled foods can be found all around the world. For example, kimchi is very popular in Korea.

June 5th is National Veggie Burger Day.

CHAPTER 5

MEATLESS MEAT

Do you know where your meat comes from? Some people choose not to eat meat. **Vegetarians** don't eat animals. **Vegans** don't eat or use animal products. This includes eggs and cheese. Some people fight for animal rights. They don't want to hurt animals.

People who don't eat meat have many options. Food scientists use plants to make meat substitutes. There are veggie burgers. There are tofu sausages. Food scientists use vegetables that have a meaty taste. Examples are jackfruit, beans, and mushrooms.

Food scientists add potatoes. Potatoes keep the **imitation** meat together. Imitation means looking like something else. Soy and wheat make the imitation meat firm. Other spices and oils are added for flavor. Food scientists use beet juice to make meat blood. They get creative.

SCIENTIST SPOTLIGHT

In 2020, Gitanjali Rao was *Time* magazine's Kid of the Year. She was 15 years old. Gitanjali is a young scientist and inventor from Colorado. She wanted to help people in Flint, Michigan. Flint had a water problem. Water is needed to live. It's more important than food. Flint's drinking water is polluted. It has high levels of lead. Lead damages the heart, kidneys, and nerves. It affects people's health. In 2017, Gitanjali invented Tethys. Tethys is a mobile device that tests lead in drinking water. It has special sensors. The sensors detect lead in water. Gitanjali said, "I don't look like your typical scientist . . . My goal has really shifted not only from creating my own devices to solve the world's problems, but inspiring others to do the same as well."

Some food scientists are making lab-grown meat. This meatless meat tastes, smells, and looks like real meat! Food scientists use real animal cells. They don't kill any animals. Instead, they take cells from their muscles or organs.

They grow these cells in a lab. They add nutrients. The cells grow quickly. They form into strips. They're stretched out. They look like meat.

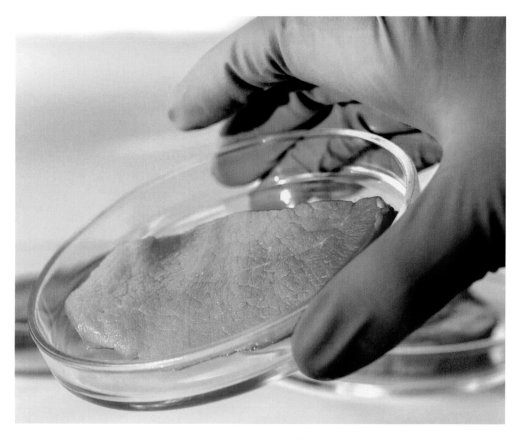

Lab-grown meat doesn't use much land. But animals raised on farms for food require a lot of land.

About 70 percent of our food in grocery stores is genetically modified.

CHAPTER 6

GMOs

Did you know you've been eating GMOs? All plants and animals have genes. Genes are parts of cells. Genes control things like looks and behavior. **Genetic codes** are instructions that tell cells how to act. These codes are passed from parents to their **offspring**. Offspring are future generations.

GMOs are **Genetically Modified Organisms**. Organisms are plants, animals, or bacteria. Modify means to change. GMOs have been changed by science. They're not natural. They're mostly used in food products. Food scientists make foods grow bigger. They make food resistant to diseases. They make food stay fresh longer.

The first GMO food to be sold in stores was a tomato.

Large crops are the most genetically modified. About 90 percent of soy, cotton, corn, and sugar beets in the United States are GMOs. These crops can survive bad weather. They last longer in storage.

Food scientists identify traits they want to keep. For example, some plants are able to fight off pests. Food scientists want other plants to have that trait. They take specific traits from an organism. They copy the traits. Then, they inject the traits into another organism. They **splice** new genes directly into an organism's genetic code. Splice means to join or connect. Food scientists give the traits to the new organism. They change the organism. Scientists can control the desired traits.

GLOSSARY

artificial (ar-tih-FISH-uhl) fake or not found in nature

bacteria (bak-TIHR-ee-uh) tiny living things that can help or hurt humans

brine (BRINE) salt water

calories (KAL-uh-rees) units of energy

canned (KAND) sealed tightly in a container

caramelizes (kar-MUH-lyze-ez) breaks down sugars into simpler sugars

coagulate (koh-AH-gyuh-layt) to change from liquid into solid

decay (di-KAY) to rot or to decompose

digested (dye-JESTED) broken down

evaporate (i-VAP-uh-rate) to turn into gas or steam

fermentation (fuhr-muhn-TAY-shuhn) the chemical breakdown of a substance by bacteria or yeast

flavors (FLAY-vuhrs) sensory impressions that include tastes, smells, sounds, and textures

hormones (HOR-mownz) natural substances that are made in the body and that influence the way the body grows or develops

genetic codes (juh-NEH-tik KOHDZ) instructions in genes that tell cells how to act

Genetically Modified Organisms (juh-NEH-tih-kuh-lee MAH-duh-fyed OR-guh-nih-zuhms) organisms changed by science, also called GMOs

imitation (i-muh-TAY-shuhn) something that is a copy of something else

molecules (MOL-uh-kyools) small units of a substance

nutrients (NOO-tree-uhnts) substances that the body needs to function, including proteins, vitamins, and minerals

papillae (puh-PIH-lee) small sensory bumps on the tongue

pickled (PIK-uhld) preserved in vinegar or brine

preserve (pri-ZURV) to save to avoid spoiling

sensory cells (SEN-suh-ree SELS) cells that send messages to the brain

splice (SPLYSS) to join or connect

starches (STARCH-ess) carbohydrates that include pasta, rice, and potatoes

sweeteners (SWEET-nuhrs) sugars

texture (TEKS-chur) how something feels

transfer (transs-FUR) to move

umami (yoo-MAHM-ee) savory or meaty taste

vegans (VEE-guhns) people who don't eat or use animal products, including eggs and dairy

vegetarians (vej-uh-TER-ee-uhns) people who don't eat meat from animals

vinegar (VIN-uh-gur) a strong acidic liquid

LEARN MORE

Hall, Megan Olivia. *Awesome Kitchen Science Experiments for Kids: 50 STEAM Projects You Can Eat!* Emeryville, CA: Rockridge Press, 2020.

Loh-Hagan, Virginia. *Food.* Ann Arbor, MI: Cherry Lake Publishing, 2021.

Loh-Hagan, Virginia. *Food Stylist.* Ann Arbor, MI: Cherry Lake Publishing, 2016.

Loh-Hagan, Virginia. *Weird Food.* Ann Arbor, MI: Cherry Lake Publishing, 2018.

Wheeler-Toppen, Jodi, and Carol Tennant. *Edible Science: Experiments You Can Eat.* Washington, DC: National Geographic Kids, 2015.

INDEX